Action Sports

Kung Fu

Bill Gutman

Illustrated with photographs
by Michael Sipe

Capstone Press

M I N N E A P O L I S

Printed in the United States of America.

Capstone Press • 2440 Fernbrook Lane • Minneapolis, MN 55447

Editorial Director   John Coughlan
Managing Editor   John Martin
Production Editor   James Stapleton

Library of Congress Cataloging-in-Publication Data

Gutman, Bill.
  Kung Fu / Bill Gutman.
    p. cm.
  Includes bibliographical references and index.
  ISBN 1-56065-267-5
  1. Kung fu--Juvenile literature. I. Title
GV1114.7.G88 1996
796.8'159--dc20   95-6410
                                                   CIP
                                                   AC

Table of Contents

Master Gin Foon Mark, a fifth-generation master, practices the Praying Mantis system of kung fu fighting.

Chapter 1

What is Kung Fu?

Kung fu means the skill or ability to do something. It can be cooking or painting or playing a musical instrument. It also can mean being skilled in the fighting arts.

Kung fu is not just one style of fighting or self-defense. There are several hundred different styles of kung fu. There are kung fu systems of fighting, health development, and even dance.

Kung fu goes back hundreds of years. That's why there are so many different styles. Whenever a master would devise a new style, he would soon have a group of devoted followers. Respect for the master has always been a strong feature of the kung fu world.

Chapter 2
Kung Fu Styles

Some of the different styles of kung fu are very unusual. Several are based on the movements of animals. Some of the most popular styles are the **Monkey style**, the **White Crane style**, and the **Praying Mantis style**.

In each case, the master who created the style watched the movements of a certain animal. The kung fu movements of each style are based on how that particular animal would defend itself in battle.

Two other popular styles are the **Drunken Man style** and the Wing Chun style. The movements of the Drunken Man style look like those of a drunken man. Even so, when done right, it's a very effective means of fighting.

Bruce Lee and Wing Chun Style

The Wing Chun style is probably the most popular form of kung fu. It also has the least dramatic movements. But it was made exciting by **Bruce Lee**. Lee brought Wing Chun-style kung fu to the movies in the 1960s and early 1970s. He made a series of successful martial arts films and became one of the best-known movie stars of his time.

Lee died in 1973. But his imitators in martial arts movies continued to use Wing Chun-style kung fu as their main fighting style.

Bruce Lee fought in the Wing Chun style of kung fu.

Chapter 3
Getting Ready

Kung fu doesn't have as many leaping and spinning kicks as tae kwon do, another system of martial arts fighting. But that doesn't mean that a good kung fu artist doesn't have to be in top physical condition. Beginners, too, should make sure they are in good shape before they begin any style of kung fu.

As with the other martial arts, beginners should do a regular **aerobic exercise**. It can be running, bike riding, swimming, or jumping rope–anything that improves your wind and general conditioning.

Strength exercises are important, too. They can include calisthenics such as pushups,

pullups, and situps. Weight training is another good idea. If you are a beginner, you should have a coach or trainer show you the best exercises to do.

Stretching

The martial arts require a loose, flexible body. Muscles must be strong, but not too tight. With all the quick movements, punches, and kicks, a tight muscle can lead to a pulled muscle. It is very important to do a lot of **stretching.**

Before each workout, be sure to stretch the muscles of your arms, shoulders, legs and back. That keeps the muscles loose and relaxed.

There are many good stretching exercises. A coach will give you a complete stretching routine to follow. A good one is the split stretch. With feet spread apart, touch one hand to the opposite toe, then repeat using the other

A skillful kung fu fughter can defend himself against powerful kicks.

Kung fu includes different attacking and defending moves, some done in combinations.

hand. Come to a full standing position in between.

The hamstring stretch is done with one leg raised up straight on a waist-high support. With the other knee bent slightly, bend at the waist and slide your hands down the outstretched leg toward the foot. Repeat with the other leg.

The hurdler's stretch loosens muscles in the backs of your legs as well as the lower back. It is done sitting down, one leg outstretched, the other bent at the knee and tucked tight to the buttocks. Bend at the waist and slide your hands toward the outstretched foot. Switch legs and repeat.

All stretching exercises should be done slowly. Hold the final stretching position for five to ten seconds. Don't stretch to a point where there is pain or discomfort. Repeat each exercise five to ten times on each side.

If stretching becames a daily part of your life, you will be able to perform any kind of kung fu to the best of your abilities. Stretching will also lessen any chance of injury.

The attacker makes three rapid blows in a row in the Praying Mantis power strike.

Chapter 4
Monkey-Style Kung Fu

Monkey Style

Monkey-style kung fu was founded in the early 19th century. There are five different divisions within the Monkey style. They are the Lost Monkey form, the Drunken Monkey, the Stone Monkey, the Standing Monkey, and the Wooden Monkey.

It takes a good coach to show you the various styles. Here are a few of the principles of each one, how they are different, and what they share.

Lost Monkey Style

In the Lost Monkey style, there is the appearance of being alone and scared. It's as if one is lost. When an enemy comes along, fear is shown by **defensive postures**. This may mean squatting close to the floor. Or it may mean rolling and tumbling to avoid attack.

But this is really a kind of act. The "lost monkey" is setting up his opponent for a **counterattack**. It may be a sudden, swift kick from the squatting position. Or the person may leap to his feet to deliver a punch or kick, then return to the defensive squatting position.

Drunken Monkey Style

In the Drunken Monkey style, the person appears drunk. He appears to stumble and lose his balance. He may stagger or roll from side to side. As in the Lost Monkey style, he stays close to the mat, squatting or rolling.

All the time his body is relaxed and watchful, waiting for a chance to attack. The attack may come with a kick or a series of punches. They may be front or side kicks.

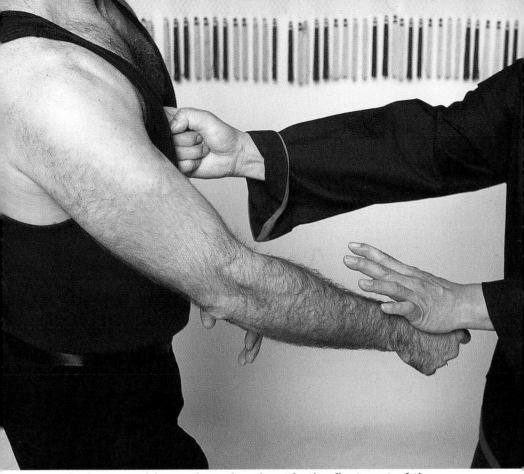

A short, rapid punch to the chest is the first part of the power strike.

When they come, they are executed with perfect balance and form.

Someone skilled in the Drunken Monkey style is very difficult to hit. He rolls with each blow, and then leaps up again to do battle. It's a strange style, but it can be very effective.

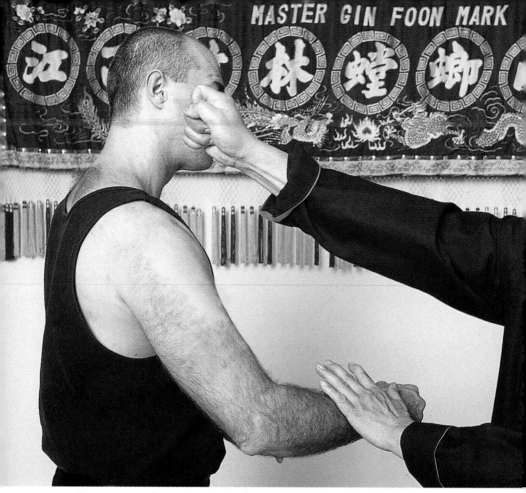

Some punches come so fast that the opponent has no chance to put up a good defense.

Wooden Monkey Style

The Wooden Monkey style is similar and also based on **deception**. It also uses a false retreat to lure opponents. Then comes a sudden attack.

Stone Monkey Style

The Stone Monkey style is more direct. The fighter meets force with force and trades blow for blow. Those who do Stone Monkey style must be able to take full blows to the body.

Standing Monkey Style

Standing Monkey is a style that is usually practiced by very tall people. A tall person might have problems with the squats and rolls of the other styles. Standing Monkey style is based on powerful, long-distance arm swings, which sometimes come out of low, deep stances.

Chapter 5

More Kung Fu Styles

White Crane Style

The White Crane style was brought to China by Tibetan monks. It is said to have been created after a monk watched an ape trying to rob eggs from a crane's next. Instead of retreating from the larger–and stronger–animal, the crane attacked fiercely. Its skill and speed finally kept the ape from taking the eggs.

A colorful lion's head is an important part of the ancient Chinese art of lion dancing.

White Crane kung fu teaches defensive or evasive tactics. You wait for the right moment before making a counterattack. But once the attack has begun, it must be kept up until there is either a victory or a defeat.

The movements imitate the movements of the crane. For striking with the fists, the entire body twists. Power comes from the small of the back. You swing your arms like the giant wings of the crane.

The fingers and thumb of your hand are held like a beak, bunched together. That way, they can "peck" at the softer, vital parts of the opponent's body. White Crane-style students learn about the **pressure points** of the body. That's where most of the punches (or pecks) are aimed.

Most of the stances for White Crane style have your legs spread far apart and your hands held away from the body. With several stances,

Master Gin Foon Mark shows his student an effective way of defense.

the student balances on one leg. Sometimes your legs are crossed, and sometimes they are evenly spread well beyond shoulder width.

Kicks can be aimed directly at an opponent, or they can be punishing, stomping motions. White Crane is not an easy style to learn. There are many different movements, and students must be strong and quick. White Crane can be a punishing form of kung fu.

Drunken Man Style

This is a very unusual style. If done correctly, it can fool an enemy and be a very powerful fighting method. Like other forms of kung fu, the drunken style is based on deceiving an enemy. The trick is to appear drunk and unsteady, sometimes falling on the ground.

But all the while, there is control. Even though he is wobbling back and forth, the "drunken man" uses a wide stance to give

Students try for an advantage using their skill and quickness.

himself balance. His arms remain in a position where he can lash out with punches. He uses his arms to block punches from the attacker.

After he blocks a punch, he can turn "drunkenly" to his left, kick backwards, and sweep the leg out from the attacker. Sometimes he will fall to the ground, only to lash out with a series of powerful kicks.

In the Drunken Man style, there is a lot of swaying back and forth and side to side. Your arms rise and fall with the body movements. There are different punches and blocking movements. There are also wrestling-type throws and a lot of fighting methods from the floor. It takes a lot of time and practice to learn the Drunken Man style well.

Praying Mantis Style

The Praying Mantis style of kung fu goes back to the 17th century. The first master of the style created it after watching a praying mantis

Praying Mantis fighters use extended arms to attack or to deflect a blow.

defeat another insect in battle. It has changed and developed over the many years since.

Most times, the hands are held in the **mantis claw**. The index and middle fingers are thrust forward. They are supported by the thumb. The two other fingers are bent back toward the wrist. This imitates the jagged "teeth" of the mantis claw. The grip is used to grab the wrist or elbow of an opponent.

As a rule, the arms are held out in front of the body to protect the chest and abdominal area from attack. The "mantis" moves smoothly and in a circle. In this style, the weaker fighter has a chance to defend himself against the stronger.

The movements of the Praying Mantis style are swift and sometimes difficult. There are punches, kicks, throwing moves, grasping, pulling, and locking of joints.

The Short Power Punch

One technique of the Praying Mantis style is the **short power punch**. This is a punch that starts about six inches (15 centimeters) from the target. You throw it with your elbow bent slightly and your wrist cocked back. The elbow is suddenly snapped forward and the fist snapped down and forward. With practice, you can generate great power with this kind of blow.

Praying Mantis style takes a long time to learn. In fact, many experts say that it takes some seven years of study and practice to become really good at it. It doesn't happen overnight.

In kung fu fighting, body strength is not as important as skill and quickness.

Chapter 6

Bruce Lee and Wing Chun Style

Wing Chun is the most widely known form of kung fu. It is the most popular Chinese martial art of all. This is due to the popularity of the late Bruce Lee and those who came after him. Even so, Wing Chun is probably the least exciting kung fu style to watch.

It doesn't have the dynamic movement of the other kung fu styles. There are no animal

Master Mark was once Bruce Lee's instructor. Lee used many of the short punches of the Praying Mantis style.

imitations, no rolling and tumbling, and no roundhouse motions of arms and legs.

In Wing Chun-style kung fu, unlike many other martial arts, defensive and offensive moves are always carried out at the same time. When the left hand is making a block, for example, the right hand may be delivering a punch. Everything is done with great speed and economy of movement.

The Straight-Line Target

The Wing Chun style concentrates on attacking the center of an opponent's body. It is almost as if there is an imaginary line from the center of the head straight down the center of the chest and abdomen. Punches and kicks are generally aimed at some point along this line.

Punches and kicks are made by short, direct blows, delivered in a **straight line** to the target.

Punches can be delivered with the fist, the fingertips, the side of the hand, or the heel of

The master counters a blow with his left hand and delivers another with the right.

the hand. Kicks are mostly the straight ahead type with no spinning or roundhouse kicks.

The Straight-Line Stance

The basic Wing Chun stance shows how compact the style is. The fists are held along the center line in front of the chest. One fist is held behind the other (sometimes the back hand is left open), as a backup for punching or blocking. The lead fist is also ready to punch or block.

Your shoulders are kept down, not hunched. Elbows are held low to protect the trunk. The hands can drop instantly to protect the groin area. Feet are shoulder-width apart.

Bruce Lee's Three-to-One-Inch Punch

This maneuver was made famous by Bruce Lee. It is a short punch delivered from a distance of one to three inches (2.5 to 7.5

Proper balance is an important part of self-defense, no matter what style you're studying.

centimeters) from the target. It is usually delivered with the fist held vertically.

The fist is propelled by strong elbow action. As it lands, it turns upwards and moves back toward the forearm. With practice and a strong final turn of the wrist, great power can be generated from this short distance.

Bruce Lee often landed rapid blows, one after another, from this short distance, sending his opponent reeling backwards.

Speed–Not Strength

You do not have to be especially strong to practice Wing Chun-style kung fu. It is a style based on speed and careful movement. It is not based on strength alone. Like other forms of kung fu, it takes time to learn.

If you want to learn kung fu, pick one style that interests you. No one can learn all of them at once. Then get yourself into good shape and find a good instructor.

The Buddha smiles on kung fu fighters who have the patience to learn and practice their skills.

Glossary

aerobic exercise–an exercise that improves general physical conditioning, especially heart-lung function. Running and bicycling are examples of aerobic exercise.

Bruce Lee–the movie star who practiced Wing Chun-style kung fu in his very successful films. Lee made Wing Chun the most popular form of kung fu.

counterattack–an attack made by someone after a first attack is made by his opponent. The counterattack is a big part of many forms of kung fu.

deception–making someone believe something that is not true. Many forms of kung fu use deception.

defensive posture–a position in which you are defending against attack. Many forms of kung fu begin with the defensive posture, from which a counterattack is launched.

Drunken Man style–a form of kung fu in which the unsteady movements of a drunken man are used as the basis of defense and attack

mantis claw–the position of the fingers and hand for the Praying Mantis style of kung fu. The index and middle fingers are thrust forward, supported by the thumb. The other two are turned back toward the wrist.

Monkey style–a form of kung fu that copies the squatting, tumbling, and rolling movements of a monkey

Praying Mantis style–a form of kung fu based on the fighting postures of the praying mantis, a large insect

pressure points–parts of the body especially vulnerable to attack

short power punch–a short, powerful punch with the fist that is part of the Praying Mantis style of kung fu. The punch travels six inches (15 centimeters) or less, but can do great damage.

straight-line target–an important part of Wing Chun-style kung fu. In Wing Chun, you usually attack the center of an opponent's body. It is as if an imaginary line runs down the center of the body from head to chest to abdomen.

stretching–extending or stretching the muscles of the body to make them stronger and more flexible. Stretching is an important part of kung fu.

White Crane style–a style of kung fu based on the movements of the white crane

To Learn More

Anderson, Robert. *The Kung Fu Book.* Las Vegas, Nev.: Pioneer Books, 1994.

Barrett, Norman S. *Martial Arts.* New York: Franklin Watts, 1988.

Chow, David and Richard Spangler. *Kung Fu: History, Philosophy, and Technique.* Burbank, CA: Unique, 1982.

Resiberg, Ken. *The Martial Arts.* New York: Franklin Watts, 1979.

Ribner, Susan and Richard Chin. *The Martial Arts.* New York: Harper & Row, 1978.

Acknowledgments

Capstone Press wishes to thank Master Gin Foon Mark of St. Paul, Minnesota for his help with this project.

Some Useful Addresses

Magazines

Black Belt Magazine
24715 Avenue Rockefeller
Santa Clarita, CA   91380

Inside Kung Fu
4201 W. Van Owen Place
Burbank, CA 91505

Index